Presented

- - - - - - - - - - -

By:

- - - - - - - - - - -

Date:

- - - - - - - - - - -

Scripture quotations marked (NIV) are taken from the Holy Bible, New International Version®. NIV®. Copyright © 1973, 1978, 1984 by International Bible Society. Used by permission of Zondervan. All rights reserved.

Scripture quotations marked (ESV) are from the Holy Bible, English Standard Version® (ESV®), copyright © 2001 by Crossway, a publishing ministry of Good News Publishers. Used by permission. All rights reserved.

Scripture quotations marked (NLT) are taken from the Holy Bible, New Living Translation, copyright © 1996, 2004, 2007 by Tyndale House Foundation. Used by permission of Tyndale House Publishers, Inc., Carol Stream, Illinois 60188. All rights reserved.

Scripture quotations marked (NCV) are taken from the New Century Version®. Copyright © 2005 by Thomas Nelson, Inc. Used by permission. All rights reserved.

Scripture quotations marked (MSG) are taken from The Message. Copyright © 1993, 1994, 1995, 1996, 2000, 2001, 2002. Used by permission of NavPress Publishing Group.

Scripture quotations marked (ISV) are taken from the Holy Bible: International Standard Version®. Copyright © 1996-2012 by The ISV Foundation. All rights reserved internationally. Used by permission.

Scripture quotations marked (CEB) are taken from the Common English Bible®, CEB® Copyright © 2010, 2011 by Common English Bible.™ Used by permission. All rights reserved worldwide.

Written by P. C. Martin
Illustrations by Anne Elisabeth
Edited by Jessie Richards

ISBN 13: 978-1-63264-048-2

© 2015 Book Barn Publishing. WA, USA
All Rights Reserved.
Printed in China.

Jesus and Me

my Body my World

My Body

Happy and Healthy	4
Four Healthy Principles	6
Food Power	8
Fabulous Fruits and Vegetables	10
Sleep and Be Strong	12
Fresh Air and Sunshine	14
Active and Energized	16
Shiny Clean	18
Play Safely	20
Super Safety Tips	22
When You're Not Feeling Well	26
Quiet and Peaceful	28
Angels Around You	30
Happier Thoughts, Healthier Life	32

My World

I Made the World!	36
All Kinds of Animals	40
Seeds to Saplings to Trees	42
Water, Water, Water	44
A Look into Outer Space	46
Habitats of Wild Creatures	48
Growing Gardens	50
Nighttime Creatures	52
Growing Food for a Whole Planet	54
The Art of Recycling	56
The Mysterious Ocean	58
Nests and Wings	60
Sun, Showers, and Snow	62
Take Care of Your Planet	64

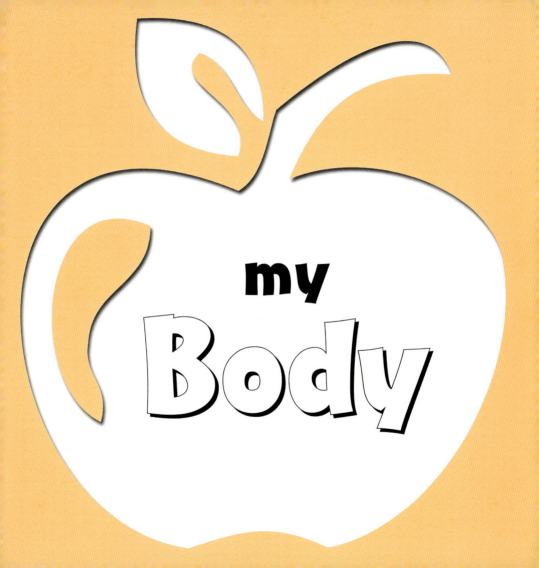

Happy and Healthy

I am the great Creator, and I created your body. It makes Me happy when you do your part to take care of My wonderful creation—you!

An important part of being happy and healthy is staying close to Me. I love to be part of your life, to participate in all the things you do. I am always happy to show you ways to take care of yourself so that you are a joyful reflection of Me. You can always turn to Me for help when you need it, because I'm always there, and I love to provide what you need.

You are God's temple and God's Spirit lives in you.

—1 Corinthians 3:16 (CEB)

Four Healthy Principles

Isn't it wonderful to be healthy, to feel strong, and to have plenty of energy? There are some basic principles I designed to help your body stay fit and healthy. These are some of the most important ones:

- Eat good, wholesome food every day. Food gives your body energy and makes you strong.
- Get plenty of sleep and rest. Sleep helps you grow and helps you stay healthy.
- Enjoy lots of exercise, especially outside in the fresh air and sunshine. Exercise helps your body in many ways.
- Keep clean. It protects you from germs and sickness.

If you do all these things, you'll be doing your part to stay healthy.

Since you know these things, you will be happy if you do them.
—John 13:17 (CEB)

Food Power

Everybody needs food, including you. Did you know that different kinds of foods have various vitamins and minerals and proteins and fiber and other nutrients that help your body in different ways? Eating healthy food gives your body what it needs for you to grow strong and healthy.

I created many interesting foods, with a variety of flavors, because I want you to enjoy your meals. It makes Me happy to see you enjoy your food, because I know that it's doing your body so much good. Remember to thank Me for providing the food, and also thank the cook.

*Whether you eat or drink or whatever you do,
you should do it all for God's glory.*

—1 Corinthians 10:31 (CEB)

Fabulous Fruits and Vegetables

For a quick and tasty, full-of-energy snack, there's hardly anything better than fruits and vegetables. A strong, healthy body eats plenty of vegetables and fruit every day. I made so many different kinds of fruits and vegetables! Bright red cherries and apples, juicy oranges and pears, delicious watermelons, little grapes and berries, fuzzy peaches, crunchy carrots, leafy greens, cool cucumbers, chewy corn, orange pumpkins, cute peas, and broccoli and cauliflower trees. Can you think of other fruits and vegetables?

Try to eat fabulous fruits or vegetables with each meal, and for snacks too. Fruits and vegetables are like wonder-foods that I've made to help you stay healthy and fit!

God said, "Look! I have given you every seed-bearing plant throughout the earth and all the fruit trees for your food."

—Genesis 1:29 (NLT)

Sleep and Be Strong

It's bedtime. You've had a big day, and the sun has gone down.

Did you know that your body needs sleep in order to grow? Sleeping helps you get taller and stronger. During your sleep, your body builds up its strength, and when you wake up, you are fit and ready for another day. Sleep also helps protect you from sickness and helps your body fix itself when it needs to. Sleep recharges your brain—like recharging a battery.

Sleep can be an adventure, too! While your body is asleep, your mind is free to dream and explore the amazing world of your imagination. Good night and sweet dreams!

When you lie down, your sleep will be sweet.
—Proverbs 3:24 (ESV)

Fresh Air and Sunshine

Take a deep breath. Now let it out slowly. You need plenty of fresh air coming in to your lungs to keep your body clean and healthy and working well inside. Your body also needs sunshine, as it gives you vitamins that help you fight sickness. When you go outside to play, your body absorbs many good things that sunlight and fresh air provide. When it's warm enough, you can also get some fresh air inside by opening the windows.

To feel fit and vigorous, breathe in as much clean, fresh air as you can, and enjoy the beautiful outdoors whenever you can.

Sunshine is sweet; it is good to see the light of day.
—Ecclesiastes 11:7 (NCV)

14

Active and Energized

I made your body to be active. Exercising keeps you healthy and fit. When your body is active, your muscles grow, your bones get stronger, your heart pumps better, your lungs take in more air, and you have more energy. Playing outdoors in My beautiful creation is an excellent way to move and exercise your body and have lots of fun. You can play at a playground, join in games and sports, run, hike in nature, walk and explore, ride a bicycle, do gymnastics, or swim! There are so many ways to get your body active and energized.

Can you think of other ways to exercise your body? What are some of your favorite ways?

The LORD is my strength.
—Exodus 15:2 (NLT)

Shiny Clean

There's nothing like a good bath to get rid of all the dirt after a long day, and it's so nice to get all clean and comfy before climbing into bed. It's good to keep clean during the day, too. There are so many things to touch and do all day long, and your hands and face sometimes get dirty. Wash your hands and face often throughout the day, and always wash them before eating and drinking. When you keep clean—when you take your shower, and wash your hands and face during the day—you are helping protect your body from the germs that might make you sick.

Let people see God in and through your body.

—1 Corinthians 6:20 (MSG)

Play Safely

The world is a wonderful place with awesome things to see and do, and I love watching you enjoy it and explore it. Sometimes, though, you'll be told to be careful. That's because some things are dangerous, especially when you're little, like climbing tall trees or big rocks or playing near a steep slope.

So, while you're having fun, you need to keep your eyes open for dangers, and avoid them. I watch out for you, and I do My part to protect you, and your part is to do your best to stay away from dangerous places and activities. Then you will have lots of fun and will be safe.

Watch your step. Use your head.
—Ephesians 5:15 (MSG)

Super Safety Tips

- Play carefully—watch out for dangerous places or things that could hurt you.

- Don't run indoors or on the stairs—you could crash into somebody or something.

- Wear safety gear when riding a bicycle or using rollerblades.

- Wear shoes when playing outside to protect your feet.

- Never touch electrical sockets or wires.

- Stay away from hot stoves, pots, or heaters. They can burn you.

- Do not play with or taste medicines or cleaning supplies—they can make you very sick!

- Keep away from broken glass and things with sharp edges. They can cut you.

- 🍓 When you're in a car, always buckle your seat belt before you leave. Be sure to stay quiet while you're on the road so you don't disturb the driver.

- 🍓 Always look both ways, and make sure the road is clear and safe, before crossing the street.

- 🍓 If you want to go in the water—a bathtub, a pool, or a pond—make sure a grown-up is watching you.

- 🍓 If you meet an animal you don't know, ask the owner if it's okay to pet the animal before you touch it.

- 🍓 Obey your parents, teachers, and caregivers when they give you safety instructions.

- 🍓 Listen to My voice in your heart and stay close to Me.

When you follow and obey these safety guidelines, it helps Me to help you stay safe.

God takes care of all who stay close to him.
—Psalm 31:23 (MSG)

Super Safety Tips

When You're Not Feeling Well

Oh dear, you've gotten sick, and now you have to stay in bed and rest. I know how that feels, because I was sick sometimes when I was a little boy. Be patient, little one, and think about how happy you'll be when you're well again.

Even though you get sick sometimes, I made your body to be healed. But you need to do the things that will help your body to get better, by resting, eating wholesome food, taking vitamins or medicine, and keeping your thoughts positive.

If you ever get lonely or bored while you are unwell, you can talk to Me. I'll be there to keep you company and help you feel better.

I am the LORD who heals you.
—Exodus 15:26 (NLT)

Quiet and Peaceful

Shhh! Get quiet for a little while. It's great fun to be active and busy, and that's very important. But sometimes you need to stop moving and be quiet and still. It's good for your body to rest and relax.

You can sit down or lie down and think about things that make you happy, and think about Me. If you're real quiet, you might be able to hear the sounds of nature. The wind, the water, the birds, and other little creatures, all have songs to sing, which you can only hear when you get quiet.

During those times, you might also hear My still, small voice in your heart, telling you wonderful things.

Be still before the LORD and wait patiently for him.
—Psalm 37:7 (ESV)

Angels Around You

Even when you do your part to stay healthy and safe, there are times when you need extra protection against sickness, accidents, or harm. I am very concerned about your well-being. So do you know what I did? I put My angels near you to help care for you.

You may not be able to see or hear or feel the angels who guard you, but they are beside you all the time. When you pray, you give them more power to protect you. Sometimes they will warn you of danger, or do other things to keep you from harm. Aren't you thankful for My wonderful angels who care for you?

[God] will order his angels to protect you wherever you go.

—Psalm 91:11 (NLT)

Happier Thoughts, Healthier Life

Did you know that being happy and grateful helps you live a healthier life? That's the truth! People who are thankful for the good things they have, and who even find reasons to be glad when they get sick or have accidents, often get better faster, and they stay healthy longer. Thinking happy, positive, joyful, thankful, and loving thoughts helps you be healthy in body and mind.

Here's a fun activity we can do together: Let's draw pictures of the things you are thankful for, and we'll see if we can fill up an entire page. That's a lot of happiness!

In everything be thankful.
—1 Thessalonians 5:18 (ISV)

my World

I Made the World!

Let Me tell you the story of how I created the universe—the sun and moon and stars, the planets, the beautiful world around you, and every galaxy in space!

Before I made the world, there was only emptiness and darkness. I created light. I created the earth and the beautiful sky above it. I made the oceans and rivers and streams. I made land appear. I covered the land with beautiful trees, plants, and flowers.

I put brilliant lights in the sky. I made the sun to shine during the day, the moon to glow during the night, and filled the sky with many twinkling stars. I filled the ocean with fish and swimming creatures, and I sent birds flying across the sky.

I created animals and creatures of every sort—from huge animals like dinosaurs and elephants and hippopotamuses to tiny creepy crawlies, furry bunnies, playful puppies, and cute kittens. I created people who could walk, run, think, talk, dance, and play.

I was pleased with how beautiful My creation turned out. I want you to have fun exploring and enjoying the wonders of the world around you and do your best to take good care of the beautiful world that I made.

God created everything.

—John 1:3 (NLT)

All Kinds of Animals

Have you seen the animals that live in the zoo? Or read books about the many kinds of animals that I have created? At the zoo, you can see animals which usually live in many different habitats. It's fascinating to learn about animals and their lives.

Imagine what it might feel like to be some of those animals. Wouldn't it be fun to be able to swing from branches like a monkey does? And can you imagine having a neck as long as a giraffe's? You would be as tall as a tree!

The animals are special creations of Mine, and I'm happy when people appreciate them, care for them, and protect their habitats.

God made all sorts of wild animals, livestock, and small animals. ... And God saw that it was good.

—Genesis 1:25 (NLT)

Seeds to Saplings to Trees

Look at the different trees around you. There are many kinds of trees, with different sizes and shapes of branches and leaves. Leaves are usually green, but sometimes they are other colors too. Some trees have fruits, and some have flowers.

Did you know that every tree grew from a seed? Yes, even the tallest tree was once nothing but a tiny seed. That's amazing, isn't it?

A newly sprouted tree is called a sapling. It takes years for a sapling to grow into a big, tall tree. Trees release fresh oxygen into the air—what you breathe every day! Trees provide shade for smaller plants, and shade for you too! Trees are important, and you can help to take care of them.

*God made all kinds of trees grow out of the ground—
trees that were pleasing to the eye and good for food.*

—Genesis 2:9 (NIV)

Water, Water, Water

People use water every day in many ways. You drink water and use it to cook your food. You use water to brush your teeth and keep your hands and face and body clean. Water is lots of fun to play and swim in.

People, animals, and plants all need water to stay healthy and even to stay alive. There are some places in the world where there isn't enough clean water for people, and they get sick. You can do your part to help by learning to save water, and not waste it. That will help there to be enough of it for everybody who needs it.

The rain and snow come down from the heavens and stay on the ground to water the earth.

—Isaiah 55:10 (NLT)

A Look into Outer Space

The sky is full of shining lights. During the day, the sunlight is so bright, you can't see any stars. But on clear nights, the stars shine like millions of candles in space. If you look carefully, you might see a meteor shooting across the sky.

A telescope helps you to see the wonders of outer space more clearly. Stars move together in groups called galaxies. Did you know that the earth is part of a galaxy called the Milky Way?

Outer space is really, really vast! But do you know what? The entire universe is not big enough to hold Me. I'm even bigger than that!

*The heavens declare the glory of God,
and the sky above proclaims his handiwork.*

—Psalm 19:1 (ESV)

Habitats of Wild Creatures

High in the mountains, strong goats leap about and eagles soar through the skies. Deep in the ground live wiggly worms and burrowing moles. Dolphins, whales, turtles, and many awesome fish live in the deep sea. Meerkats and lizards make their homes in shady dens in the desert. Ducks and swans live by rivers, lakes, and ponds. Polar bears love the freezing snow and icy ocean. Moose and deer inhabit leafy forests. Little sparrows and finches create homes in hollows and tree branches.

Each animal is different, and each is a part of this amazing earth. Respect the habitats which I have provided for the creatures of your planet.

Every animal of the forest is mine. … I know every bird in the mountains, and the insects in the fields are mine.

—Psalm 50:10–11 (NIV)

Growing Gardens

Planting a garden can be fun. Keeping a garden is hard work, too, because gardens need a lot of care. You need to dig up the ground, plant the seeds, water them, and keep bugs, birds, and bunnies from eating the little plants. You must dig up the weeds and keep the ground healthy. Most of all, you must have patience, because it takes time for plants to grow and blossom.

Vegetable gardens provide delicious fresh food. Flower gardens are beautiful to look at, and bees use the pollen from the flowers to help other plants grow.

There is plenty you can learn when you work with nature. Taking care of a garden can be a wonderful experience.

God said, "Let the land sprout with vegetation—every sort of seed-bearing plant."… And that is what happened.

—Genesis 1:11 (NLT)

Nighttime Creatures

After the sun has set and you're getting ready for bed, if you could see in the dark, you'd notice something interesting happening outside. When it's dark, many creatures wake up and crawl out of their cozy daytime beds, rested and ready for action.

There are badgers, foxes, raccoons, owls, and many other animals that fill the night with activity. They can see in the dark. They gather their food, eat, and play all night long.

When the sun rises, it's bedtime for all those creatures, and they creep back into their dens and nests to sleep. These nighttime creatures are some of the many different and interesting animals I made, and they have their special place in your world.

In [God's] hand is the life of every creature.
—Job 12:10 (NIV)

Growing Food for a Whole Planet

There are so many different kinds of food! Different countries around the world have their own special foods. Wherever you live, most of the food you eat comes from places called farms, which grow your food.

The farmers plant seeds and care for the crops. Then when the crops are fully grown, they are harvested, transported, stored, and distributed, and finally used to cook delicious meals.

Growing enough food for everyone is a big and important job. You get vegetables, fruits, grains, meat, milk, and eggs from farms.

Your body needs food in order to grow and be healthy. Be thankful for the farmers and for your food. Take care not to waste it.

[God] makes grass grow for the cattle, and plants for man to cultivate—bringing forth food from the earth.

—Psalm 104:14 (NIV)

The Art of Recycling

"Recycling" is a big word that means using something old to create something new. In My creation, everything is recycled naturally. When plants die, they decay into the ground and are absorbed into the soil, and new plants grow from that soil. You can recycle things that people make, too, by putting old things to good use, and by disposing of trash properly. Clever people have discovered ways of turning many kinds of garbage into various useful things.

When you put all your garbage into its proper place, and recycle, you are helping to keep the earth clean and beautiful.

If you are faithful in little things, you will be faithful in large ones.
—Luke 16:10 (NLT)

The Mysterious Ocean

Oceans cover more of the earth than land does. The oceans are more than just water. You can find amazing creatures, plants, and landscapes in the amazing underwater world that I created. Different kinds of wildlife inhabit different parts of the ocean, depending on whether the water is warm or cold, shallow or deep.

You can travel across the ocean by ship, or explore its depths in a submarine. Even if you spent your whole life exploring the ocean, there would still be new things to discover.

The ocean and its wonders are a very special and valuable part of nature, and it is each person's responsibility to keep it clean and to protect its treasures.

God created the great creatures of the sea and every living and moving thing with which the water teems.

—Genesis 1:21 (NIV)

Nests and Wings

Think about some of the many birds in the world. There is the colorful macaw, the waddling penguin, the singing nightingale, the graceful albatross, the skillful kingfisher, the busy hummingbird. Each bird is special in its own way. Some birds fly and others can't; some birds build complicated nests while others live in a hollowed hole in a tree.

No matter what the type of bird, I created each one perfectly for its habitat, whether it's the wintery arctic or the hot desert, the wet rain forest or the craggy mountains. Each one has what it needs. And just as I take care of the littlest sparrow, I promise to take care of you.

Look at the birds. They don't plant or harvest or store food in barns, for your heavenly Father feeds them.

—Matthew 6:26 (NLT)

Sun, Showers, and Snow

Did you know that the sun is always shining? You can't always see it, though, when there are clouds and when it rains or snows. Both sunshine and rain are important to life on earth. The sun gives light, warmth, and energy. The rain helps plants and food to grow and provides water for people and animals. When it gets very cold, rain sometimes freezes and turns into snow.

The sunshine, the rain, the wind, and even the snow are necessary for the earth and its people. I made them all and make them work together the way they need to.

I will send you rain in its season.

—Leviticus 26:4 (NIV)